GRAPHIC NATURAL DISASTERS

HURRICANES

by Gary Jeffrey

illustrated by Mike Lacey

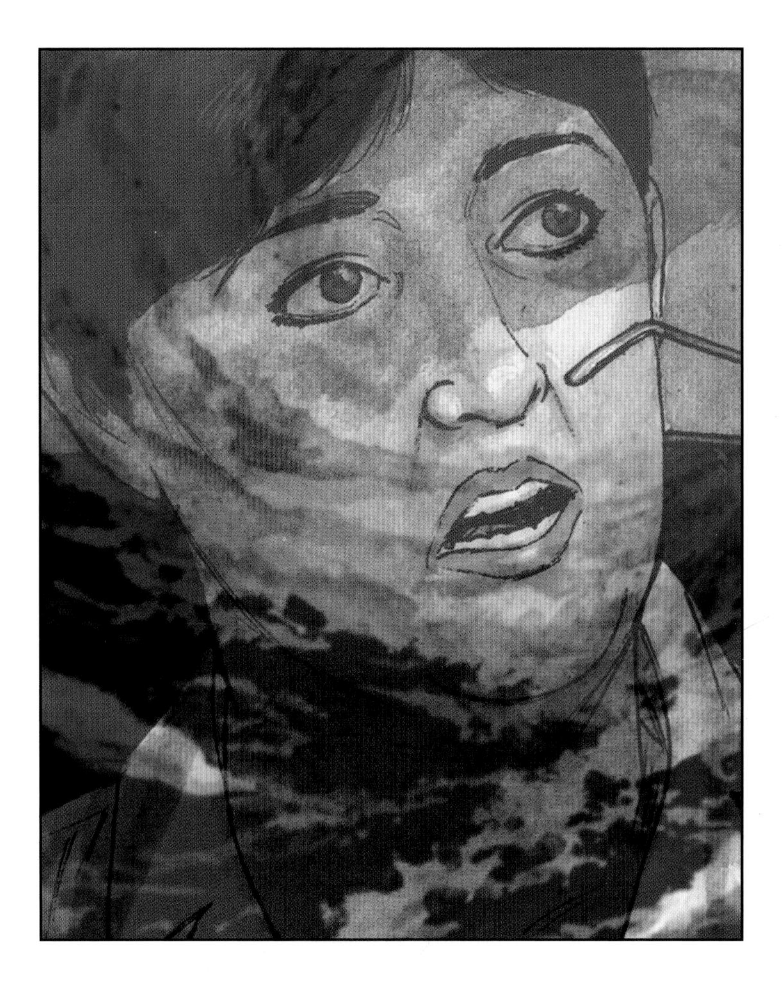

FRANKLIN WATTS
LONDON•SYDNEY

First published in 2010 by Franklin Watts

Franklin Watts
338 Euston Road
London NW1 3BH

Franklin Watts Australia
Level 17/207 Kent Street
Sydney, NSW 2000

A CIP catalogue record for this book is available from the British Library.

Dewey number: 363.3'4922

ISBN: 978 0 7496 9257 5

Franklin Watts is a division of Hachette Children's Books, an Hachette UK company.
www.hachette.co.uk

GRAPHIC NATURAL DISASTERS: HURRICANES produced for Franklin Watts by
David West Children's Books, 7 Princeton Court, 55 Felsham Road,
London SW15 1AZ

Designed and produced by
David West Children's Books

Editor: Gail Bushnell

Photo credits:
p4/5t&m, NOAA; p5b, Historic NWS collection; p44/45all, NOAA

Printed in China

Website disclaimer:
Note to parents and teachers: Every effort has been made by the Publishers to ensure that the websites in this book are suitable for children, that they are of the highest educational value, and that they contain no inappropriate or offensive material. However, because of the nature of the Internet, it is impossible to guarantee that the contents of these sites will not be altered. We strongly advise that the Internet is supervised by a responsible adult.

CONTENTS

WHAT IS A HURRICANE? 4

HOW ARE HURRICANES FORMED? 6

THE GREAT LABOR DAY HURRICANE OF 1935 8

HURRICANE ANDREW, 1992 17

HURRICANE KATRINA, 2005 30

OBSERVING & STUDYING 44

GLOSSARY AND THE SAFFIR-SIMPSON SCALE 46

FOR MORE INFORMATION 47

INDEX 48

WHAT IS A HURRICANE?

A hurricane is a severe tropical storm that forms over the sea in the Atlantic and Pacific oceans. In different parts of the world, this type of storm has other names.

Although, in effect, they are all the same thing, severe tropical storms are called by different names depending on where they occur in the world.

VIOLENT AND DANGEROUS

Most hurricanes die out at sea. Sometimes they make landfall and bring with them chaos and destruction. A hurricane produces huge waves called storm surges, heavy rain, flooding and violent winds, up to 290 km/h, accompanied by tornadoes. Hurricanes can be as big as the United States but the largest ones are not necessarily the most powerful. Hurricane Andrew was quite small but caused over $20 billion of damage in 1992. Hurricanes are measured from 1 to 5 by the Saffir-Simpson scale (see page 46).

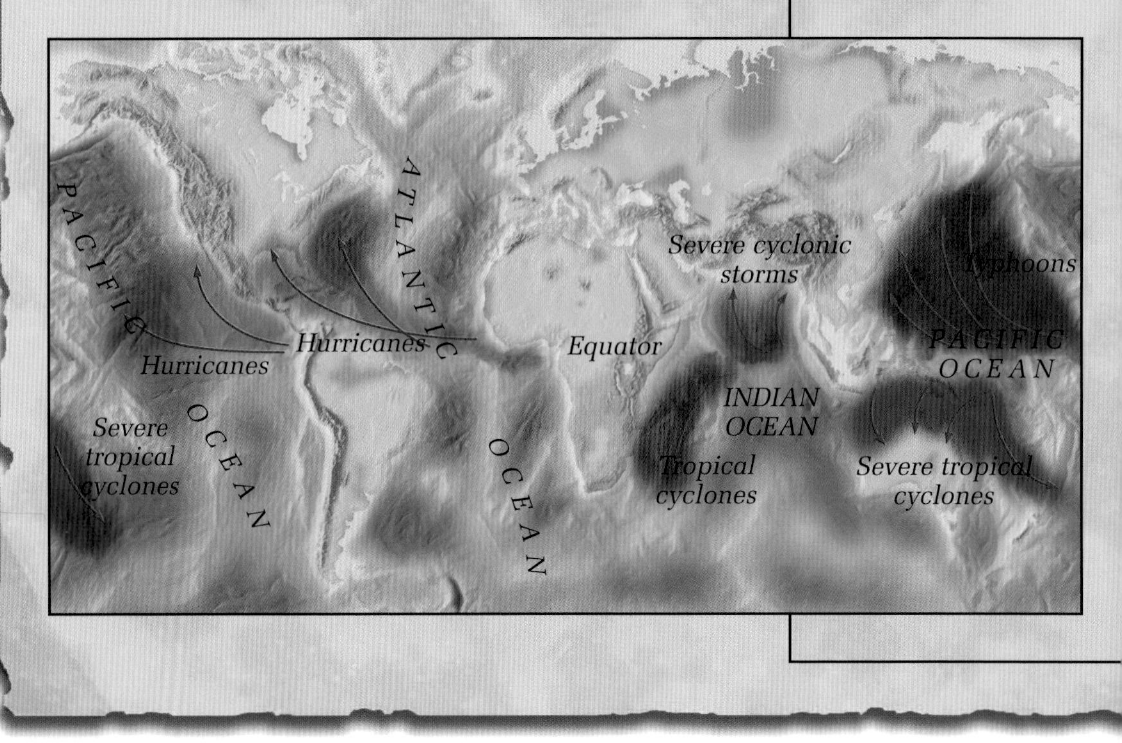

Storm surges caused massive flooding in New Orleans and surrounding Louisiana coastal areas when Hurricane Katrina hit the city in 2005. The aerial photograph (left), shows the streets close to the damaged Superdome, a large sports arena.

Violent winds during Hurricane Andrew caused huge damage to man-made structures and nature. A wooden stake was driven through a Royal Palm (left), while housing was completely destroyed (below).

HOW ARE HURRICANES FORMED?

Most hurricanes begin near Africa's west coast, above the equator, and move westwards.

Spinning Clouds

Water vapour rises from a warm sea and starts to form clouds. The air pressure falls and more air moves in to equalise the air pressure. The Earth's spinning affects the air movement and the clouds begin to rotate in a counter-clockwise motion. This is known as the Coriolis effect.

Fuelling the System

As the clouds rise, they cool and rain falls. This releases heat, which warms the surrounding air, and the air pressure drops further. More air is drawn in and the cloud system becomes wider and deeper.

Hurricane

The storm gets bigger. When wind speeds reach 119 kilometres per hour, a storm officially becomes a hurricane. At this stage, it is given a name. Hurricanes can vary in size, but are typically 500 kilometres wide. At the centre is a clear area of calm, which can be up to 60 kilometres wide, called the eye.

1. *Clouds form over a warm sea and a low pressure area forms. As air is drawn in it rotates due to the Coriolis effect. At this stage the system is a tropical depression.*
2. *Rainfall fuels the low pressure area and the storm builds. The system becomes more circular in shape and as winds hit 62–117 km/h it is called a tropical storm.*
3. *The system becomes a hurricane. A cutaway shows pillars of storm clouds that spiral into the centre. The wind spins faster towards the centre and up the wall of the 'eye'. Air from the top falls down the walls of the eye. In front of the hurricane is a high wave called a storm surge.*

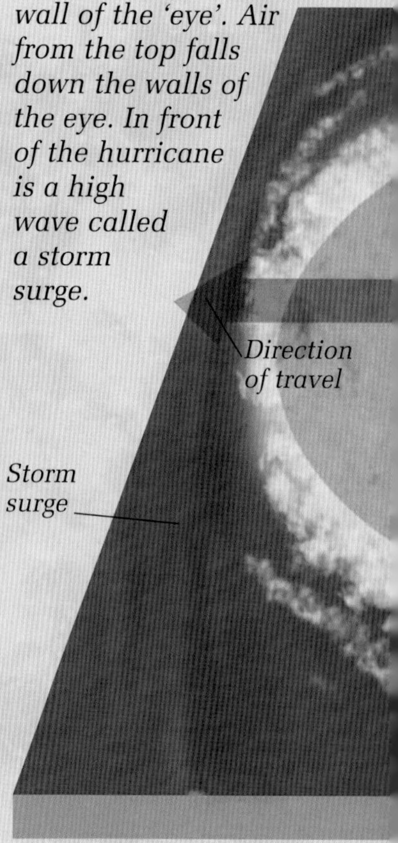

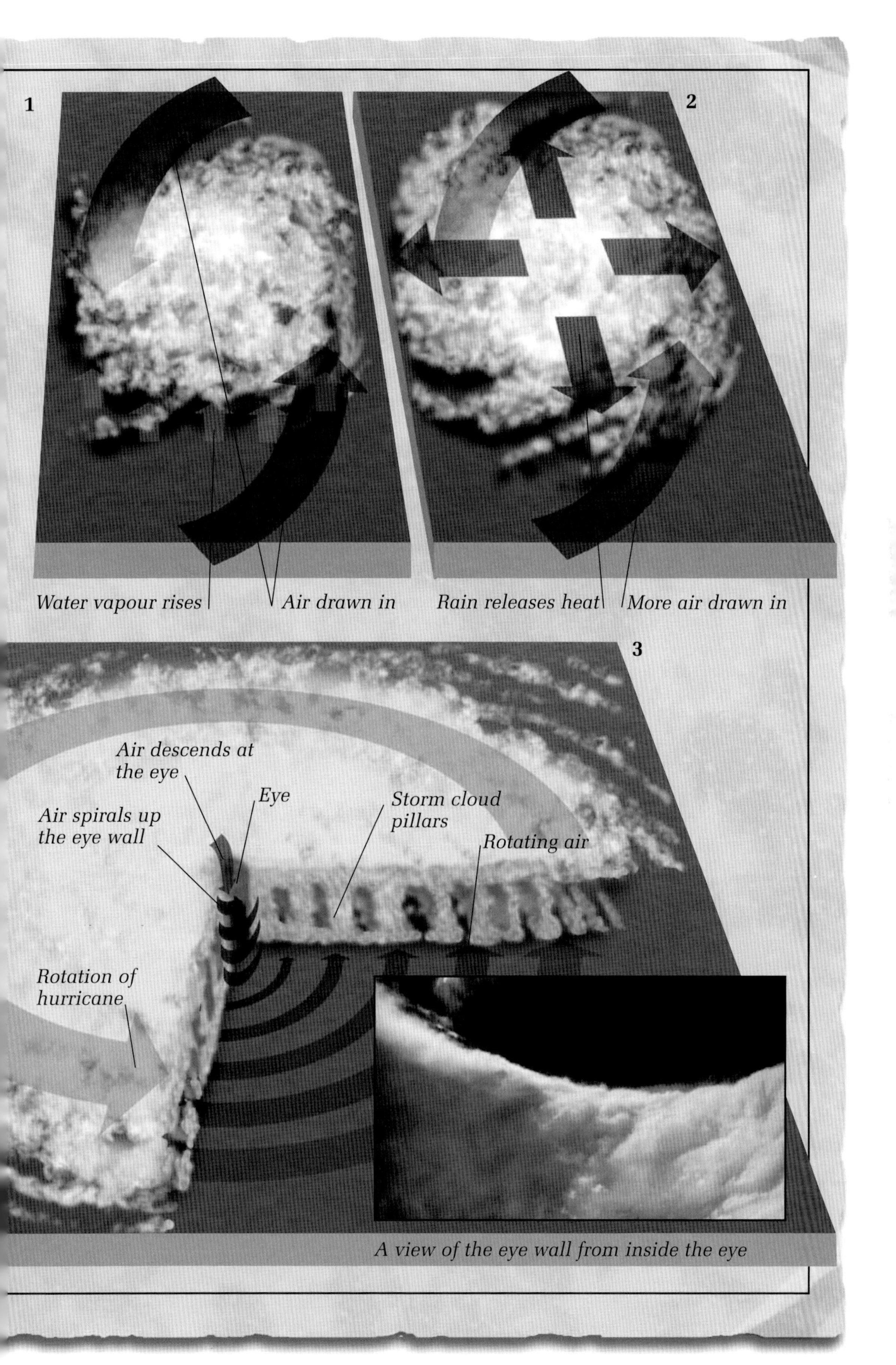

A view of the eye wall from inside the eye

THE GREAT LABOR DAY HURRICANE OF 1935
ISLAMORADA, UPPER MATECUMBE KEY, FLORIDA, 2 SEPTEMBER 1935, 9:00 AM.
SO, YOU DIDN'T WANT TO GO TO MIAMI WITH THE OTHERS?
NOT ME, I GET TRAIN SICK!
JIM LINDLEY AND GEORGE HILL ARE TWO OF 650 WAR VETERANS WHO HAVE COME TO BUILD A NEW HIGHWAY TO LINK THE FLORIDA KEYS.
DID YOU HEAR ABOUT THE STORM WARNING ISSUED YESTERDAY?
YEAH, I ASKED THE LOCALS AND THEY DON'T SEEM TOO CONCERNED ABOUT IT.

PROBABLY NOTHING TO WORRY ABOUT THEN. I'LL SEE YOU LATER AT CAMP 3*.
*ON LOWER MATECUMBE KEY
BY 1:00 PM...
ALREADY IT'S HARD TO STAND UP IN THIS WIND AND THE STORM'S NOT EVEN HERE YET!
I'M GOING TO SEE THE SUPER, I THINK THEY NEED TO GET US OUT.
OKAY! OKAY! CALM DOWN. WE'VE ALREADY WIRED HOMESTEAD TO SEND AN EVACUATION TRAIN. IT SHOULD BE HERE IN AN HOUR.
OFFICE
HOMESTEAD, 72 KILOMETRES TO THE NORTH...
RELIEF TRAIN?
DON'T THEY KNOW WE'RE SHUT DOWN FOR THE HOLIDAY?

THIS IS HOMESTEAD, WE'VE GOT SOME SORT OF EMERGENCY DOWN ON THE KEYS. I WAS WONDERING...
MEANWHILE, ON MATECUMBE KEY, JOHN HENRY RUSSELL HAS GATHERED HIS FAMILY TOGETHER...
THIS LOOKS AS IF IT'S GOING TO BE A BAD STORM.
THE RUSSELLS ARE LOCAL LIME GROWERS.
I THINK WE SHOULD ALL MOVE TO THE PACKING HOUSE ON THE EAST SIDE WHERE IT'S MORE SHELTERED.
THE RUSSELLS HAVE WEATHERED MANY STORMS ON THE KEYS BUT...
I'VE GOT A BAD FEELING ABOUT THIS ONE.
MIAMI STATION, 2:35 PM.
OKAY! SO THEY'VE GOT A HURRICANE BEARING DOWN ON THEM...

...IT'S STILL GOING TO TAKE AT LEAST TWO HOURS TO GET A TRAIN READY!
ISLAMORADA, 4:00 PM...
AAAGH! THERE'S NOWHERE TO HIDE FROM THIS. WHERE'S THAT TRAIN?
32 KILOMETRES NORTH OF ISLAMORADA, 6:50 PM...
COME ON, LET'S GO! WE'VE GOT TO GET TO MATECUMBE KEY!
I'LL GO AS FAST AS I CAN, BUT THESE CONDITIONS - THEY AREN'T SAFE!
447
AT ISLAMORADA, THE WIND IS BLOWING SAND AROUND JIM LINDLEY SO HARD...

...THAT IT CREATES ENOUGH STATIC TO CATCH FIRE!
AAAAAAGH!

AT THE PACKING HOUSE...
926
THE BAROMETER'S GONE SO LOW...
RAIN
FAIR
DRY
...IT'S DROPPED OFF THE SCALE!
FATHER...

708
...THERE'S SALTWATER RISING.

STORM SURGE! WE'VE GOT TO GET TO HIGHER GROUND!

BUT, FATHER, THE WIND!
JUST HOLD ON TO SOMEONE AND DON'T LET GO!
WHEN THEY HEAD OUTSIDE...
NOOOO!

MOTHER!

CAMP 3, LOWER MATECUMBE KEY, 8:22 PM. GEORGE HILL IS SEEKING SHELTER.
...MUST...GET...TO...THE... SUPPLY BUILDING!
WAAAAGH!
CRASH!
A FIVE-METRE SEA SURGE, DRIVEN BY THE HURRICANE, LASHES THE LOW-LYING KEY.
MEANWHILE AT ISLAMORADA...
ALL ABOARD!

ROOOAAAR
WHAT THE...?!
THE RELIEF TRAIN HAS ARRIVED TOO LATE. THERE IS NO ESCAPE.
HIIIISSSSSSSSS!

THE SURVIVORS FIND SHELTER IN THE WRECKAGE.

TWO DAYS LATER, RELIEF ARRIVES AND GEORGE HILL AND JIM LINDLEY ARE RESCUED. OVER 423 PEOPLE, INCLUDING 259 CAMP VETERANS, HAVE PERISHED IN THE SMALL BUT INCREDIBLY INTENSE HURRICANE.

THE LABOR DAY HURRICANE STILL HOLDS THE RECORD FOR THE LOWEST RECORDED BAROMETRIC PRESSURE FOR A LANDFALLING US STORM AT 66.92 CM OF MERCURY.

THE END

HURRICANE ANDREW, 1992
INTERSTATE 75, FLORIDA. SUNDAY, 23 AUGUST, US AIRFORCE PILOT BOB FOZNOT IS GIVING OUT-OF-STATE VISITOR NENA WILEY A RIDE FROM MIAMI TO SARASOTA.
SO, FUZZY, DID YOU HEAR? THEY POSTED A HURRICANE WATCH FOR SOUTH FLORIDA.
SURE, BUT IT'S NOTHING TO WORRY ABOUT–THE STORM'S OVER 500 MILES AWAY...
...AND THESE HURRICANES ARE USUALLY PUSHED NORTH WAY BEFORE THEY HIT US.
SARASOTA, 12:15 PM. NENA HAS ARRANGED TO MEET HER FRIEND, EDDA.
HERE'S FINE.
EDDA'S TRAVEL CORNER
NEWS
...AND NOW BREAKING NEWS...

...EVACUATION OF POPULATED AREAS, FROM KEY WEST UP TO FLORIDA CITY, HAS BEGUN AS A PRECAUTIONARY MEASURE...
HMM...ARE YOU GOING TO GO ON UP TO TAMPA LIKE YOU PLANNED?
NO, I THINK I'LL CALL THE BASE*, GAS UP THE VAN AND HEAD BACK TO MIAMI.
*HOMESTEAD AIRFORCE BASE, MIAMI
AND YOU?
I'M GOING TO PHONE CHRISSI FROM EDDA'S.
CHRISSI IS NENA'S 16-YEAR-OLD DAUGHTER. SHE IS STAYING WITH HER BEST FRIEND IN SOUTH DADE COUNTY, SOUTH OF MIAMI.
MOM! IT'S SO EXCITING! WE'RE UNDER A HURRICANE WARNING. EVERYONE'S BEEN ORDERED TO EVACUATE!
HANG ON A MINUTE, CHRISSI...
CLICK!
SINCE THIS MORNING THE HURRICANE HAS ACHIEVED CATEGORY FOUR STRENGTH–WINDS OF UP TO 155 MPH...

AND NOW, THE EYE OF HURRICANE ANDREW IS AIMED DIRECTLY AT THE BAHAMAS AND SOUTH FLORIDA.
HURRICANE WARNING
CHRISSI, I'M COMING BACK RIGHT NOW! IN THE MEANTIME, I WANT YOU TO GO TO THE GRAVERS' HOUSE IN WEST KENDALL, OKAY?
WEST KENDALL'S FURTHER INLAND. NOW, LET'S SEE IF I CAN GET A FLIGHT BACK.
THEY'VE SHUT DOWN MIAMI AIRPORT! EDDA – HOW MUCH GAS DO YOU HAVE IN YOUR CAR?
YOU THINK WE CAN STILL CATCH UP TO FUZZY?
INTERSTATE 75, HEADING SOUTH...
COME ON, FUZZY, WHERE ARE YOU?
NENA, IF I TAKE YOU ANY FURTHER I WONT HAVE ANY GAS TO GET HOME!
UNDERSTOOD. JUST TAKE ME AS FAR AS THE STATE 41 TOLL.
I'LL BE ABLE TO HITCHHIKE FROM THERE.
SPEED LIMIT 15

THE HOUSE OF BEN AND ANN HORENSTEIN, KENDALL, SOUTH DADE...
I'VE FINISHED TAPING THE WINDOWS, HONEY.
THESE FLASHLIGHTS ARE ALL GOOD.
I'VE LASHED THE PROPANE TANKS TO THE BIG OAK TREE.
AND I'VE MOVED THE CAR TO THE EAST SIDE OF THE HOUSE, SO IT WON'T GET TOTALLED IF THE GARAGE BLOWS IN.
STATE 41, 96 KILOMETRES FROM WEST KENDALL...
GEE, THANKS FOR GIVING ME A RIDE.
IT SEEMS LIKE THE WHOLE OF SOUTH DADE IS HEADING NORTH.
FORD
THEY HAVEN'T HAD A MAJOR HURRICANE STRIKE HERE FOR OVER 20 YEARS.
MAYBE TIME'S FINALLY RUN OUT FOR SOUTH FLORIDA.

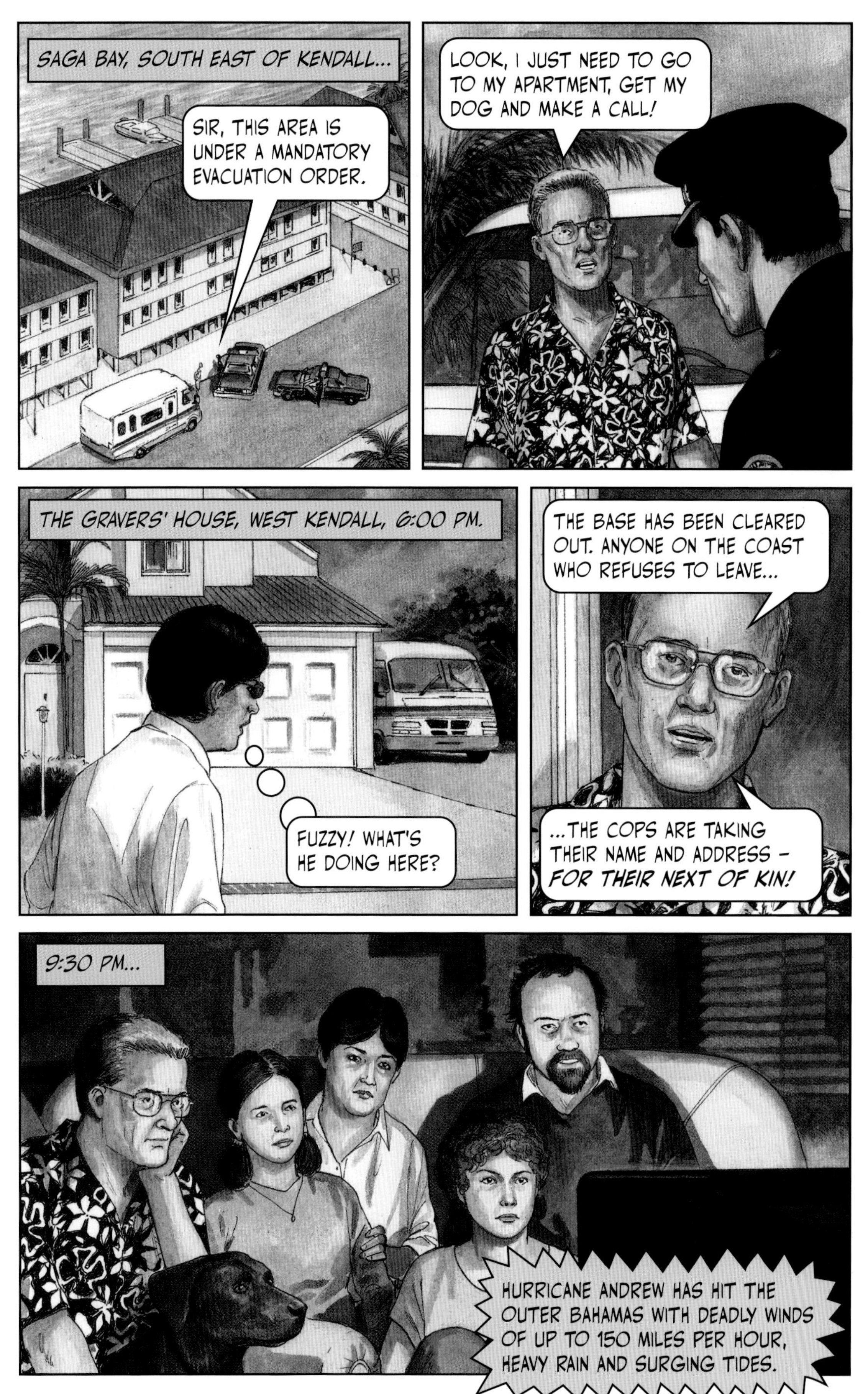
SAGA BAY, SOUTH EAST OF KENDALL...
SIR, THIS AREA IS UNDER A MANDATORY EVACUATION ORDER.
LOOK, I JUST NEED TO GO TO MY APARTMENT, GET MY DOG AND MAKE A CALL!
THE GRAVERS' HOUSE, WEST KENDALL, 6:00 PM.
FUZZY! WHAT'S HE DOING HERE?
THE BASE HAS BEEN CLEARED OUT. ANYONE ON THE COAST WHO REFUSES TO LEAVE...
...THE COPS ARE TAKING THEIR NAME AND ADDRESS – FOR THEIR NEXT OF KIN!
9:30 PM...
HURRICANE ANDREW HAS HIT THE OUTER BAHAMAS WITH DEADLY WINDS OF UP TO 150 MILES PER HOUR, HEAVY RAIN AND SURGING TIDES.

IT'S LIKELY THAT THE STORM WILL STRENGTHEN TO JUST UNDER A CATEGORY FIVE AS IT CROSSES THE GULF STREAM TO HIT SOMEWHERE IN SOUTH FLORIDA.
WE'RE GOING TO SEE SOMETHING DOWN HERE THAT I HOPED I WOULD NEVER EXPERIENCE. WHEREVER THE CENTRE HITS WILL BE *LEVELLED*. THIS IS GOING TO BE **THE WORST!**
THE HORENSTEINS', 12:00 AM...
DAD! I'M SCARED!
POWER'S OFF! I'LL GO AND CHECK THE CIRCUIT BREAKER.
?

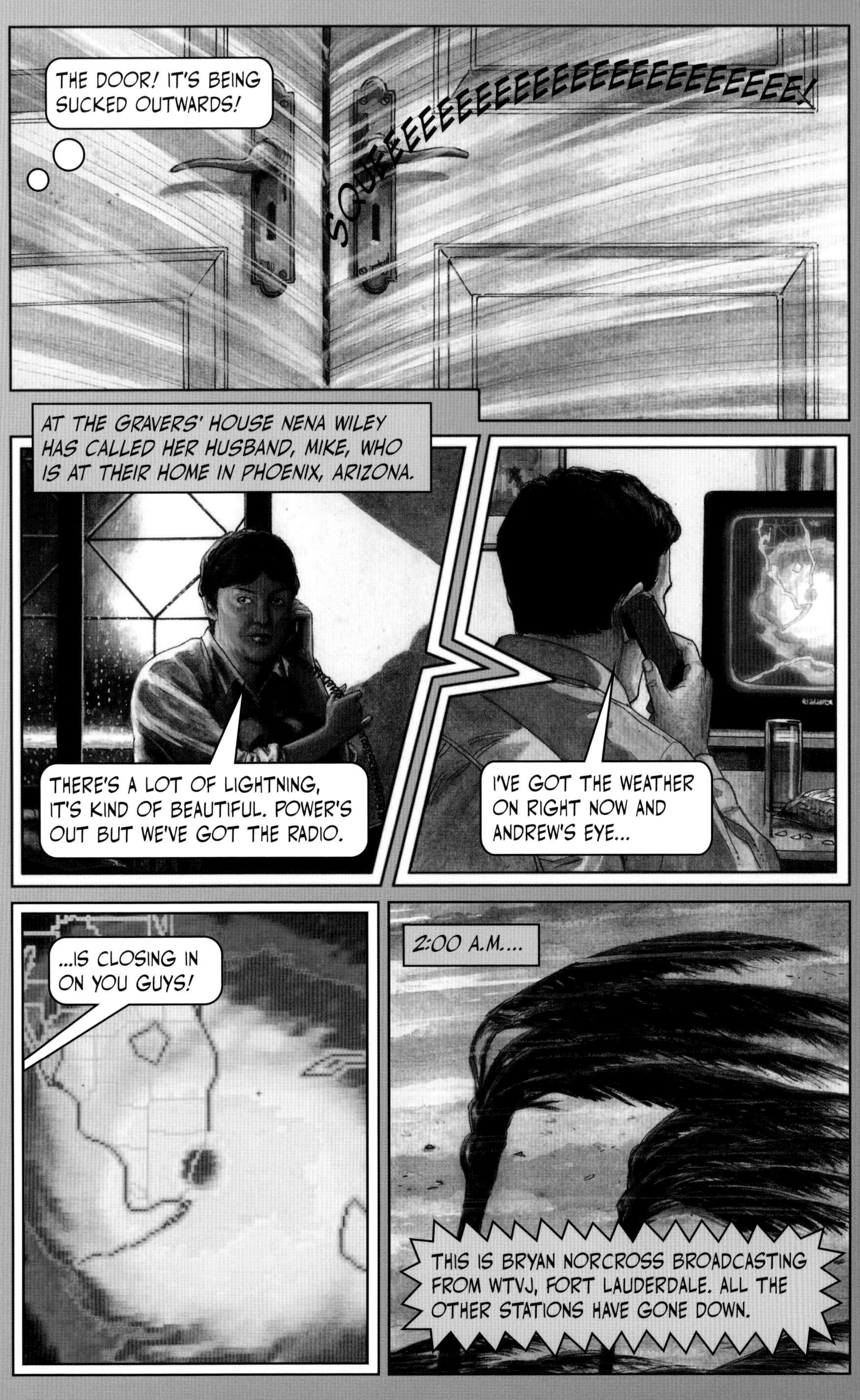
THE DOOR! IT'S BEING SUCKED OUTWARDS!
SQUEEEEEEEEEEEEEEEEEEEEEEEE!
AT THE GRAVERS' HOUSE NENA WILEY HAS CALLED HER HUSBAND, MIKE, WHO IS AT THEIR HOME IN PHOENIX, ARIZONA.
THERE'S A LOT OF LIGHTNING, IT'S KIND OF BEAUTIFUL. POWER'S OUT BUT WE'VE GOT THE RADIO.
I'VE GOT THE WEATHER ON RIGHT NOW AND ANDREW'S EYE...
...IS CLOSING IN ON YOU GUYS!
2:00 A.M....
THIS IS BRYAN NORCROSS BROADCASTING FROM WTVJ, FORT LAUDERDALE. ALL THE OTHER STATIONS HAVE GONE DOWN.

ANDREW IS NEARLY UPON US. WE WILL STAY ON THE AIR AS LONG AS...
KRAAAAARRRK!!
OH, NO! THE POOL DOME!
KRAAAAAKWAAAAAAARRRK!!!
GET AWAY FROM THE WINDOWS!
LET'S GET SASHA IN THE BATHROOM!
COME ON!...WHAT IS IT, GIRL?
BOOOOOOM!

AAAAGH! MY EARS ARE POPPING
ROOOOOAAAARRRR.
IT'S THE PRESSURE DROP - EVERYONE GET IN THE HALL!
HANG ON FUZZY!
GNAAGH! I CAN'T HOLD THEM!
I CAN HEAR MORE WINDOWS GOING! LET'S JUST PRAY THE ROOF STAYS ON!

THE HORENSTEINS'...
SKEEEEEEEEEWAAAAAAAAAAR!
...BLESSED BE THE NAME OF HIS GLORIOUS KINGDOM FOREVER AND...
WE'RE GONNA BE OK, WE'RE GONNA BE...
...STAY UNDER THE BLANKETS, I'M GOING TO SEE WHAT THAT SOUND IS!
CRACKK! CRACKK!
CRACKK! CRACKK!
BOOHOOOOM!
AAAAGH!
RIP! RIP! RIP!
OH NO, THE ROOF!

THE GRAVERS'...
THE RADIO!
ZZT...THIS IS WTVJ, THE TIME IS 2:30 AM.
THE EYE OF HURRICANE ANDREW IS EXPECTED TO MAKE LANDFALL AT AROUND 5:00 AM ON THE COAST NEAR HOMESTEAD, BUT THIS ISN'T WHERE THE STRONGEST WINDS WILL BE.
THEY WILL BE AROUND THE NORTHEASTERN EYE WALL, DIRECTLY OVER KENDALL. FEROCIOUS WINDS OF OVER 165 MILES PER HOUR, MAYBE OVER 200 IN GUSTS.
ANDREW IS A SMALL HURRICANE. ITS DESTRUCTIVE WINDS ONLY REACH OUT 30 MILES FROM THE EYE.
BUT ANDREW *IS* MOVING FAST, SO SEEK REFUGE AND COVER YOURSELF WITH A MATTRESS...IT *WILL* BE OVER SOON!

THE HORENSTEINS', 5:30 AM...
BENNY? ANN?
MR LUBIN?
THANK GOODNESS YOU ALL MADE IT!
AT THE GRAVERS'...
WE'RE ALL ALIVE, BUT OH MY!

OUTSIDE...
SO MANY HOUSES DESTROYED...
...AND ALONGSIDE, OTHERS HARDLY DAMAGED AT ALL.
HOW COULD ANDREW'S WINDS BE SO...FICKLE?
THE CATEGORY FIVE STORM WINDS CONTAINED MINI-TORNADOES, WHICH OBLITERATED ANYTHING IN THEIR PATHS.
ANDREW WAS HERE
26 PEOPLE DIED AND OVER $25 BILLION WORTH OF DAMAGE WAS CAUSED. HURRICANE ANDREW IS THE SECOND MOST EXPENSIVE NATURAL DISASTER IN THE HISTORY OF THE UNITED STATES.
THE END

HURRICANE KATRINA, 2005

SUNDAY, 28 AUGUST, 6:00 AM. TROPICAL CYCLONE KATRINA, WHICH HAS MADE LANDFALL ONCE ALREADY IN FLORIDA, AS A CATEGORY ONE HURRICANE, IS NOW BACK OVER THE SEA AND HEADING FOR THE GULF COAST OF THE UNITED STATES.

WE'RE ABOUT TO GO THROUGH THE EYE WALL. EVERYBODY STRAP IN.

WOW!
THE EYE MUST BE 30 MILES ACROSS!
THEY ARE HEADING TO THE CENTRE OF THE HURRICANE'S EYE TO DROP A PROBE.
OKAY, FIX IT HERE!
THE DROPSONDE PROBE WILL SEND BACK VITAL INFORMATION ABOUT THE HURRICANE.
GET READY FOR ANOTHER PASS.

THE NATIONAL HURRICANE CENTER IN MIAMI...
OKAY, LATEST DATA ON KATRINA. WINDS: 165 MILES PER HOUR, PRESSURE: 906. SHE'S BECOME A CATEGORY FIVE!
OH BOY, AND SHE'S GETTING BIGGER AS WELL. TIME TO UPDATE THE AUTHORITIES.
EAST NEW ORLEANS, LOUISIANA, 2:00 PM...
WE ARE FACING A STORM THAT MOST OF US HAVE LONG FEARED...
...IT IS MY GRAVE DUTY TO ORDER THE MANDATORY EVACUATION OF NEW ORLEANS. PLEASE! GET OUT OF THE CITY!
ARE WE LEAVING TOWN, MOMMA?

SINCE MAYOR NAGIN'S ANNOUNCEMENT, ALL ROUTES OUT HAVE BEEN BUMPER TO BUMPER, WHILE INTERSTATE RAIL AND BUS SERVICES HAVE BEEN SHUT DOWN.
NO, WE'RE STAYING PUT.
BUT, MOMMA, WILL WE BE IN DANGER?
I DON'T KNOW, SON, I DON'T KNOW.
LATASHA ALLEN IS 27 YEARS OLD. HER FAMILY DOESN'T OWN A CAR.
MAYOR NAGIN HAD THIS ADVICE FOR ANYONE LEFT BEHIND...
ANYBODY WHO IS STILL IN THE CITY SHOULD SEEK REFUGE IN THE SUPERDOME!

WINDSOR HOTEL, GRAVIER STREET, BY THE FRENCH QUARTER...
THE STORM SURGE WILL MOST LIKELY TOPPLE OUR LEVEE SYSTEM, DROWNING THE CITY. THE SUPERDOME IS ABOVE SEA LEVEL...
...TAKE AT LEAST FIVE DAYS WORTH OF FOOD AND WATER WITH YOU. WE HAVE NO WAY OF KNOWING EXACTLY WHEN...
MELISSA PHILLIP IS A PHOTOGRAPHER SENT BY THE HOUSTON CHRONICLE TO COVER THE STORM.
THE BUSINESS DISTRICT, 9:00 PM...
NOT FAR NOW...
...JUST A FEW MORE BLOCKS.

THE LATEST FORECAST IS THAT KATRINA WILL VEER **EAST** AFTER MAKING LANDFALL EARLY TOMORROW. AT LEAST NEW ORLEANS WILL BE SPARED A **DIRECT** HIT FROM THE CATEGORY FIVE HURRICANE'S **145 MILE PER HOUR WINDS...**
THE SUPERDOME, MONDAY, 29 AUGUST, 6:00 AM.
JUST LISTEN TO THAT WIND BLOW!
6:10 AM, BURAS, LOUISIANA...
6:30 AM, NEW ORLEANS...

AT THE SUPERDOME...
KAAABOOOM!
OH, NO! THE ROOF!
6:50 AM, A SIX-METRE SURGE GENERATED BY THE STORM WINDS REACHES THE INDUSTRIAL CANAL, EAST OF THE CITY.

7:45 AM, THE FLOOD WALL AND LEVEE ON THE EAST SIDE OF THE INDUSTRIAL CANAL GIVE WAY, FLOODING THE LOWER NINTH WARD.

GRAVIER STREET, 8:00 AM...
IT'S NO GOOD - WE CAN'T DO THIS YET, LET'S GET BACK INSIDE!

9:30 AM, THE FLOOD WALLS ON THE EAST SIDE OF THE LONDON AVENUE CANAL NEAR MIRABEAU FAIL...
9:45 AM, A LARGE SECTION OF LEVEE ON THE 17TH STREET CANAL IN LAKEVIEW IS BREACHED.
JACKSON SQUARE, FRENCH QUARTER, 3:00 PM...
HOUSTON CHRONICLE
THERE'S NO STANDING WATER HERE. WE NEED TO GET TO WHERE THE FLOODING IS.
LOOK!
BOATS! LET'S FOLLOW THOSE GUYS!

ST CLAUDE AVENUE BRIDGE, THE INDUSTRIAL CANAL, NORTH BYWATER.
OH, MY! THE ENTIRE LOWER NINTH IS UNDER WATER!
MELISSA PHILLIP, FOR THE HOUSTON CHRONICLE. WOULD IT BE POSSIBLE TO HAVE JUST ONE RIDE OUT IN A BOAT SIR?
HELP US!
PLEASE HELP!
WE NEED TO RESCUE THE TRAPPED PEOPLE FIRST!

SUPERDOME, TUESDAY, 30 AUGUST, FLOOD SURVIVORS HAVE BEEN ARRIVING.
HUNDREDS HAVE JUST BEEN...WASHED AWAY.

IT ISN'T MUCH BETTER HERE, THERE'S BEEN NO WATER SUPPLY SINCE YESTERDAY MORNING!

GULFPORT, MISSISSIPPI...
MY WAREHOUSE...
SEAFO
THE MISSISSIPPI COAST HAS BEEN SWAMPED BY AN EIGHT-METRE FLOOD SURGE.
...IT'S GONE!
WEDNESDAY, 31 AUGUST 9:00 AM, MELISSA PHILLIP HAS COME TO CHECK OUT THE SUPERDOME.
I THINK THIS IS AS DEEP AS IT GOES.
MORE THAN 20,000 PEOPLE HAD GATHERED AT THE SUPERDOME...
...BUT WHY ARE THEY ALL STANDING OUTSIDE IN THE SUN?
THIS WAY, LADY.
GAAAH, OH MAN!
RETCH!

THIS IS A HUMANITARIAN DISASTER!

OUTSIDE THE SUPERDOME...
EVERY DAY, THEY SAY THE BUSES ARE COMING. BUT WHERE ARE THEY?!
PEOPLE ARE DYING HERE!
IF THEY DON'T GET US OUT, WE'RE ALL GOING TO DIE HERE!
WELL, I'M NOT WAITING AROUND TO DIE!
PHYLLIS JOHNSON HAS BEEN IN THE SUPERDOME SINCE SUNDAY NIGHT.
WHERE ARE YOU GOING?
I DON'T KNOW...BUT ANYWHERE'S BETTER THAN HERE!

THURSDAY, 1 SEPTEMBER. WHEN THE EVACUATION OF THE SUPERDOME GETS UNDERWAY, LATASHA ALLEN'S FAMILY IS ON THE FIRST BUS OUT.
MELISSA PHILLIP HAS GONE TO THE NEW ORLEANS CONVENTION CENTRE TO CHECK OUT REPORTS OF SURVIVORS THERE.
HEY! MEDIA!!
YOU MUST HELP US. WE RAN OUT OF WATER THREE DAYS AGO!
FOR PITY'S SAKE HELP US! PEOPLE ARE DYING HERE!
WHERE'S THE NATIONAL GUARD? THE POLICE? DON'T THEY KNOW ABOUT THESE PEOPLE?
SATURDAY, 2 SEPTEMBER...
YESTERDAY, THEIR PLIGHT WAS HIGHLIGHTED BY THE MEDIA. TODAY, MILITARY CONVOYS ARE AT LAST BRINGING FOOD AND WATER TO THE CONVENTION CENTRE SURVIVORS...

IT'S BEEN FIVE DAYS SINCE KATRINA STRUCK. 80 PERCENT OF NEW ORLEANS IS UNDER WATER. MORE THAN 1,800 PEOPLE HAVE LOST THEIR LIVES.

THE GULF COAST HAS BEEN DEVASTATED. HURRICANE KATRINA'S DAMAGE TOTAL EXCEEDS $75 BILLION - THE MOST EXPENSIVE STORM IN THE HISTORY OF THE UNITED STATES.

PHYLLIS JOHNSON EVENTUALLY GOT A RIDE ON A STOLEN TRUCK AND MADE HER WAY TO HOUSTON, TEXAS.

SINCE THE DARK DAYS OF SEPTEMBER 2005, MANY RESIDENTS HAVE RETURNED, DETERMINED TO REBUILD THEIR LIVES IN THE CITY THEY CALL THE BIG EASY.

THE END

OBSERVING & STUDYING

The hot and humid months of July, August and September are the peak of the hurricane season. While most people get ready to batten down the hatches, some prepare to fly into the eyes of the storms.

Hurricane Chasers

Scientists need to study these storms to predict their patterns and intensity more accurately. Specially equipped planes, able to withstand the violent winds, fly through the storms taking measurements. One instrument, called a dropsonde, is dropped from three kilometres into the centre of the eye. A parachute opens and a transmitter sends back information about wind speed, temperature, humidity and air pressure. This data, together with satellite data, helps meteorologists predict hurricanes' movements.

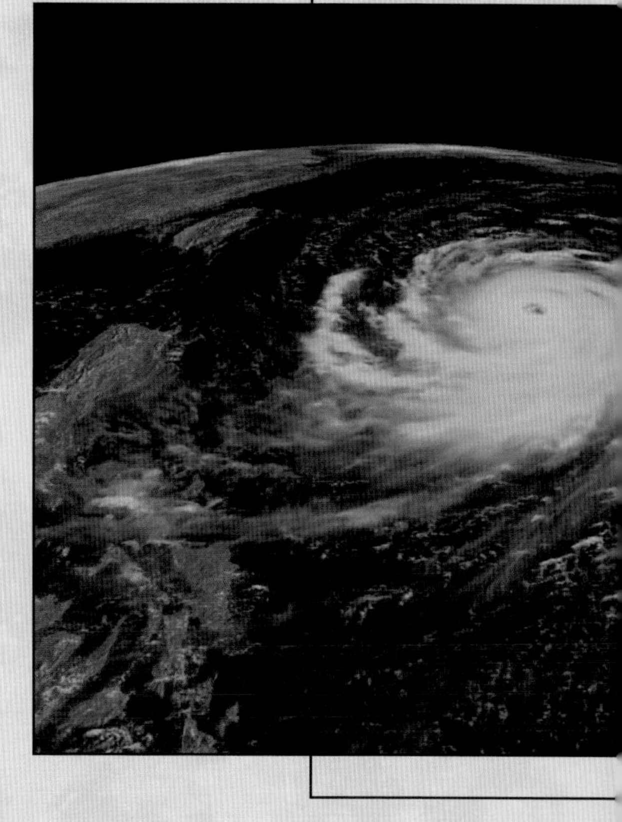

Eyes in Space

Satellites provide important information on developing storms. Meteorologists also use images from satellites to monitor a hurricane's movements. Today, plenty of advanced warning time is given for hurricanes that are likely to make landfall.

A P-3 (left) flies over the eye of Hurricane Caroline taking measurements with instruments such as the gust probe (seen above on the DC-6) and dropsondes.

Between June and November, the US National Hurricane Center in Miami keeps a 24-hour watch on satellite data. Today's high-tech imagery from satellites such as NOAA-10 (left top) and GOES (left bottom) can provide high-definition pictures of these giant storms every 15 minutes. This super typhoon in the Pacific, off the coast of Japan, had wind speeds in excess of 257 km/h, and was monitored by a GOES-9.

GLOSSARY

air pressure The weight of air due to gravity acting on its mass. When an area of air heats up it expands and becomes lighter and therefore has a lower air pressure than the surrounding cooler air. This is known as a 'low'.

barometer An instrument that measures atmospheric pressure. Barometers are used to help forecast the weather.

fickle Changeable.

humanitarian Concern for people's welfare.

mandatory evacuation The enforced moving of people from one area to another because of a danger.

meteorologist A scientist who studies and predicts the atmosphere and its weather.

obliterate To destroy something completely.

predict Saying what will happen in the future.

static Electricity created by particles of dust or grit rubbing against each other.

storm surge A rise in the sea level, moving forwards in front of a storm, which causes coastal flooding when it hits land.

tornado A rotating funnel cloud that reaches from the base of a supercell thunderstorm cloud to the ground. Wind speeds can reach up to 500 kilometres per hour.

The Saffir-Simpson Scale

Category	Winds	Effects
One	119–152 km/h	No real damage to building structures. Damage primarily to unanchored mobile homes, shrubbery and trees. Also, some coastal road flooding and minor pier damage.
Two	154–177 km/h	Some roofing material, door and window damage to buildings. Considerable damage to vegetation, mobile homes and piers. Coastal and low-lying escape routes flood 2–4 hours before arrival of centre. Small craft in unprotected anchorages break moorings.
Three	179–209 km/h	Some structural damage to small residences and utility buildings with a minor amount of curtainwall failures. Mobile homes are destroyed. Flooding near the coast destroys smaller structures with larger structures damaged by floating debris. Terrain lower than 1.5 metres above sea level may be flooded inland 13 kilometres or more.
Four	211–249 km/h	More extensive curtainwall failures with some complete roof structure failure on small residences. Major erosion of beach. Major damage to lower floors of structures near the shore. Terrain continuously lower than 3 metres above sea level may be flooded requiring massive evacuation of residential areas inland as far as 10 kilometres.
Five	>249 km/h	Complete roof failure on many residences and industrial buildings. Some complete building failures with small utility buildings blown over or away. Major damage to lower floors of all structures located less than 5 metres above sea level and within 457 metres of the shoreline. Massive evacuation of residential areas on low ground within 8–16 kilometres of the shoreline may be required.

FOR MORE INFORMATION

ORGANISATIONS

National Hurricane Center
11691 SW 17th Street
Miami, Florida 33165-2149
Website: http://nhc.noaa.gov/

FOR FURTHER READING

Challoner, Jack. *Hurricane & Tornado* (Eyewitness). London, England: Dorling Kindersley, 2004.

Connolly, Sean. *Storms* (In Time of Need). London, England: Franklin Watts, 2004.

Dineen, Jacqueline. *Hurricanes and Typhoons* (Natural Disasters). London, England: Franklin Watts, 2002.

Gemmell, K. *Storms and Hurricanes* (Usborne Understanding Geography). London, England: Usborne Publishing, 2000.

Langley, Andrew. *Hurricanes, Tsunamis, and Other Natural Disasters* (Kingfisher Knowledge). London, England: Kingfisher, 2006.

Orme, David. *Hurricane Season*. London, England: Evans Brothers, 2008.

Spilsbury, Louise and Richard. Awesome Forces of Nature: *Howling Hurricanes*. London, England: Heinemann, 2004.

INDEX

A

air pressure, 6, 25, 44, 46
Allen, Latasha, 40, 42
Atlantic ocean, 4

B

barometer, 12, 46

C

category, of storm, 18, 22, 29, 30, 32, 35, 46
Coriolis effect, 6
cyclone, 30

D

damage, cost of, 4, 29, 43
dropsonde probe, 31, 44

E

eye, the, 6, 7, 19, 23, 27, 30, 31, 45

F

fickle, 29, 46
Foznot, Bob, 17

G

Graver family, 19, 21, 23, 27, 28
Great Labor Day Hurricane, 8, 9, 10, 11, 12, 13, 14, 15, 16

H

Hill, George, 8, 14, 16
Horenstein family, 20, 22, 26, 28
humanitarian, 40, 46
Hurricane Andrew, 4, 5, 17, 18, 19, 20, 21, 22, 23, 24, 25, 26, 27, 28, 29
Hurricane Katrina, 5, 30, 31, 32, 33, 34, 35, 36, 37, 38, 39, 40, 41, 42, 43
hurricane season, 44
hurricane watch, 17

J

Johnson, Phyllis, 41, 43

L

landfall, 4, 16, 27, 30, 35, 44
Lindley, Jim, 8, 11, 16

M

mandatory evacuation, 21, 32, 46
meteorologist, 44, 46

O

obliterate, 29

P

Pacific ocean, 4, 45
Phillip, Melissa, 34, 38, 39, 42
predict, 44, 46

R

Russell family, 10

S

Saffir-Simpson scale, 4, 46
satellites, 44, 45
static, 12, 46
storm surge, 4, 5, 6, 12, 14, 34, 36, 39, 46

T

tornado, 4, 29
typhoon, 45

W

Wiley, Chrissi, 18, 19
Wiley, Nena, 17, 18, 23